NEXT STATION 2

CLIL BOOK

Ana Elisa Martins

macmillan education

CONTENTS

	SUBJECT	THEME	LANGUAGE	MY LEARNING GOALS
UNIT 1 LET'S DANCE! PAGES 4-9	**PE**	Dances	• dance expressions (clap your hands, jump, move your hips, run, stamp your feet, stand up, turn around, walk) • folk dance (semba, hoop dance, haka) • Folk dance is a traditional and recreational way to express the culture of a people. • Clap your hands. / Jump. / Move your hips.	Compare and contrast folk dances around the world
UNIT 2 WHAT TIME IS IT? PAGES 10-15	**Math**	Quantities and Measurements	• daily routines (get up, have breakfast, go to school, have lunch, have dinner, go to sleep) • analogue clock (minute hand – big hand, hour hand – small hand, dash) • digital clock (digits, colon) • 12-hour clock (am / pm) and 24-hour clock • I get up at seven o'clock. / Mary spends 6 hours at school.	Read and record time using analogue and digital clocks
UNIT 3 CLASSIFYING ANIMALS PAGES 16-21	**Science**	Life and Evolution	• animals (ladybug, cow, goat, duck, mosquito, giraffe, butterfly, zebra, donkey, chicken, sheep, caterpillar, dog, bird, snake, turtle, fish) • animal characteristics and classification: body covering (fur, feathers, scales, shell); place they live (terrestrial, aquatic); physical structure (vertebrates, invertebrates); feeding habits (carnivores, herbivores, omnivores) • Dogs have fur. / The snake has scales. / It is a (carnivore) / an (invertebrate). / It is (terrestrial).	Describe and compare animals based on specific characteristics
UNIT 4 WHERE DOES FOOD COME FROM? PAGES 22-27	**Geography**	The World of Work	• food (beans, carrots, cookies, French fries, hamburgers, ice pops, onions, pancakes, peppers, potatoes, sandwiches, tomatoes) • crop cultivation, livestock farming • food crops (grains, seeds and nuts, vegetables, fruits, herbs and spices) • animal products (meat, eggs, milk, wool) • What animals do you want to raise? / What plants do you want to cultivate?	Identify foods that come from nature
UNIT 5 MAKE-BELIEVE WORLD PAGES 28-33	**Art**	Theater	• make-believe actions (fly, do taekwondo, play the guitar) • theater features: visual language (sets, costumes, images, light); sounds (music, noises, voices); body language (gesture, movements, expressions); verbal language (scripts, lines) • A theater is a place where a play is performed. • Sometimes, I pretend I can fly. / My friend likes to pretend he can play the guitar.	Represent objects and facts through images or texts
UNIT 6 IT'S TIME TO RELAX PAGES 34-39	**History**	Public and Private Spaces	• free time activities (listen to music, play board games, read books, draw, dance, watch TV, play soccer, do puzzles) • public spaces (parks, squares, beaches, museums) and private spaces (houses) • leisure activities in the past and now • She likes listening to music. • … is a public space. / … is a private space.	Understand the difference between public and private spaces

UNIT	SUBJECT	THEME	LANGUAGE	MY LEARNING GOALS
UNIT 7 WHERE DO YOU LIVE? PAGES 40-45	**Geography**	Our Place in the World	• places to live (house, castle, apartment, boat, trailer, cave) • the country (fields, forests, farms, country houses, crop cultivation, livestock farming) • the city (streets, stores, buildings, industry, trade, services, parks, movie theathers, sports complexes) • He / she lives in a / an … • There aren't many streets, stores, or factories. / There are many people from different origins.	Recognize differences between societies
UNIT 8 LISTENING TO MUSIC PAGES 46-51	**Art**	Music	• instruments (trumpet, violin, drums, recorder, tambourine, guitar, piano) • music genres (rock, country, dance, Latin music) • Music is an important form of art and culture. • I usually listen to music to … • She is playing the …	Identify different genres and uses of music
UNIT 9 NUMBER LINE PAGES 52-57	**Math**	Numbers	• numbers from ten to one hundred • number line (straight line, numbers written in order, regular intervals, number sequence, marks) • addition and subtraction on a number line (jump spaces forwards, jump spaces backwards, decompose a number, skip count on the number line) • There are 60 buses. • This number line goes up in 2s / 5s / 10s. • How much will she spend? / How many cookies are left?	Order numbers on a number line and use it for addition and subtraction
UNIT 10 MY COMMUNITY PAGES 58-63	**History**	Where We Live	• adjectives (big, long, small, old) • clothes (hats, pants, shirts, skirts) • communities (a traditional community, a community by the sea, a farming community, urban communities) • Their traditional clothes are colorful. • It's a small / big community. • Lobitos is a small town on the north coast of Peru. / It is a very big city.	Learn about the formation of culture in societies

·ICONS·

LOOK AND DO
Activities to interpret the picture of the unit opener pages

LISTEN
Audio tracks to practice listening skills

THINK

BE

LEARN

ACT

COLLABORATE / COMMUNICATE

UNIT 1

LET'S DANCE!

PE

Check (✓) the folk dance.

UNIT 1

PE

1 Write.

clap your hands | jump | move your hips | run
stamp your feet | ~~stand up~~ | turn around | walk

1  stand up

2  ______________

3  ______________

4  ______________

5  ______________

6  ______________

7  ______________

8  ______________

2 Play Simon Says.

TRACK 1

3 Listen and number.

Folk Dance

Folk dance is a traditional and recreational way to express the culture of a people. Dance involves **body movements** (1) combined with **music** (2). People practice folk dance at **festivals** (3), funerals, marriages, religious ceremonies, and other social occasions. The dances have different themes and are passed on to **younger generations** (4).

Think Twice

1 Complete.

1 Folk dance is one of the ways to express the ______________ of a particular people.

2 People dance at ______________________, like funerals, marriages, and festivals.

2 Do you know any folk dances? Which one(s)?

UNIT 1

PE

TRACK 2

4 Listen, match, and say.

Examples of Folk Dance

Semba is a traditional type of dance and music from Angola. The word "semba" means "a touch of the bellies". Semba can express stories of everyday life and a lot of different emotions. The dance is usually in pairs, it's energetic, and you need to move your hips a lot!

Hoop dance is an indigenous North American individual dance. Many tribes from Canada and the USA practice this dance. They walk and spin one or more hoops. The hoop represents the never-ending cycle of life, because it has no beginning or end.

Haka is a ceremonial dance performed by the native people of New Zealand, the Maoris. Haka is danced in groups and it is marked by the rhythmic stamping of the feet on the ground. Maoris see Haka as a way to celebrate life.

1 
Semba

2 
Hoop dance

3 
Haka

a 

b 

c 

Think Twice

1 Read and write *se* (semba), *ho* (hoop dance), or *ha* (haka).

This dance represents

the never-ending cycle of life. ◯

a way to celebrate life. ◯

stories of everyday life. ◯

2 Are any of these dances popular in your country?

5 Research a folk dance. Complete the chart.

country	
traditional dance	
purpose	
instruments used	
body movements	

6 Draw and dance!

UNIT 2

·WHAT TIME IS IT?·

MATH

What time is it?

It's ________ o'clock.

UNIT 2

MATH

1 Look at the pictures. Complete the sentences.

~~get up~~	have dinner	go to sleep
have lunch	have breakfast	go to school

1 I get up at seven o'clock.

2 I ______________ at ______________ o'clock.

3 I ______________ at ______________ o'clock.

4 I ______________ at ______________ o'clock.

5 I ______________ at ______________ o'clock.

6 I ______________ at ______________ o'clock.

TRACK 3

2 Listen and read.

Analogue Clocks

Analogue clocks have two hands: the **minute hand** and the **hour hand**.

The **small hand** is the **hour**. The **big hand** is the **minute**. Each **dash** on the clock means **1 minute**. There are 5 minutes between each of the big numbers.

When telling the time, always look at the hour hand first. Look at the clock. The small hand points to the 5. The big hand points to the 12. It's 5 o'clock!

Digital Clocks

Digital clocks have digits like 0, 1, 2, etc. The time is written using four digits. The hours and the minutes are separated by a colon.

The hours are **on the left** side of the colon. The minutes are **on the right**. Look at the clock. It's 10 o'clock!

12-hour and 24-hour Clocks

An **analogue clock** is a **12-hour clock**. The first 12-hour period is called **am**. It runs from 12:00 midnight to 11:59 in the morning. The second 12-hour period is called **pm**. It runs from 12:00 noon until 11:59 at night.

A **digital clock** is a **24-hour clock**. It's a continuous period of 24 hours. The **24-hour clock** uses the numbers 00:00 to 23:59. Midnight is 00:00.

1 hour = 60 minutes
1 day = 24 hours

3 Complete the chart.

12-hour clock	24-hour clock
1 pm	13:00
	21:00
5 pm	

4 Do you prefer an analogue or a digital clock to read the time?

5 Match.

1 The hour hand is — a 24-hour clock.

2 The minute hand is — small.

3 An analogue clock is — a 12-hour clock.

4 A digital clock is — big.

6 Read, write, and draw.

1 I go to school at eight twenty.

2 I go to bed at nine ten.

7 Look and write.

Mary's Routine

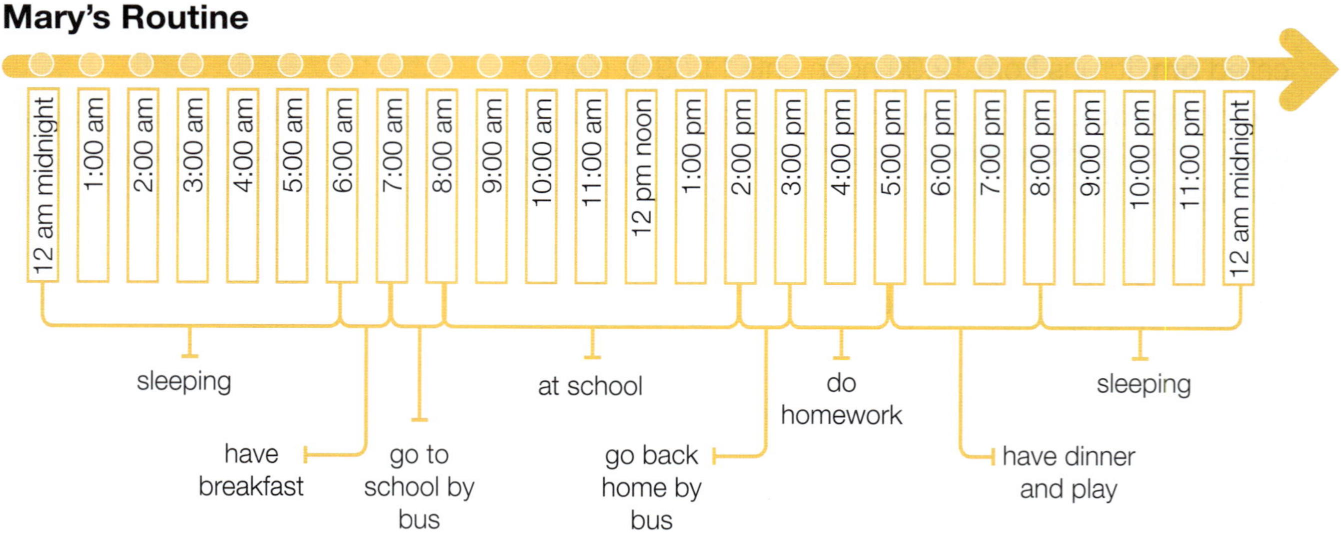

1 Mary gets up at _____ am.

2 Mary spends _____ hour on the bus to school.

3 Mary spends _____ hours at school.

4 Mary goes to bed at _____ pm.

Write your own sentence about Mary's routine.

____

_______________________________________.

8 Complete the chart with your routine.

activity	time		duration
get up	:		
have breakfast	:	:	
go to school	:	:	
at school	:	:	
	:	:	
	:	:	
do homework	:	:	
go to sleep	:	:	

9 Share your routine with a classmate.

UNIT 3

CLASSIFYING ANIMALS

Look and check (✓) the animals in the picture.

chicken ◯ elephant ◯

cow ◯ bird ◯

UNIT 3

SCIENCE

1 Find and circle the words. Then write.

l	a	d	y	b	u	g	t	o	n
c	o	w	g	u	i	y	s	h	c
s	v	u	r	t	d	y	h	f	a
g	u	b	g	t	o	k	e	d	t
o	p	a	i	e	n	n	e	c	e
a	d	b	r	r	k	u	p	h	r
t	u	f	a	f	e	w	w	i	p
j	c	k	f	l	y	s	o	c	i
s	k	i	f	y	x	d	w	k	l
o	e	z	e	b	r	a	y	e	l
d	r	b	n	w	r	q	y	n	a
m	o	s	q	u	i	t	o	l	r

1 

ladybug

2 

____

3 

____

4 

____

5 

____

6 

____

7 

____

8 

____

9 

____

10 

____

11 

____

12 

____

TRACK 4

2 Listen, say, and color the animals in Activity 1.

TRACK 5

3 Listen and read.

Animal Characteristics and Classification

There are many different kinds of animals on Earth. Animals that have things in common are called a **species**.

To study species better, scientists divide animals into groups, according to some of their characteristics, such as **body covering** and the **place they live**. This process is called **classification**.

Body covering

Animals have different coverings on their bodies. Their coverings protect them and help them survive in their habitat. There are four basic types of animal covering: **fur**, **feathers**, **scales**, and **shell**.

Dogs have fur.

Birds have feathers.

Snakes have scales.

Turtles have a hard shell.

Place they live

Animals can be **terrestrial** or **aquatic**. **Terrestrial animals** live predominantly on **land**. **Aquatic animals** live in the **water** most of the time and depend on it for survival.

Zebras are terrestrial animals.

Fish are aquatic animals.

Think Twice

1 Read and circle.

Animals can be divided into groups. True / False

Birds have scales. True / False

Terrestrial animals live on land. True / False

2 Can you name two other aquatic animals?

UNIT 3

SCIENCE

4 Cross out (✗) the one that's different. Then complete.

1 

They have fur.

2 

They have ________.

3 

They have a ________.

4 

They have ________.

TRACK 6

5 Listen and read. Then number.

Animals can also be classified according to their **physical structure** and their **feeding habits**.

Physical structure

Animals that have a backbone are called **vertebrates** (1). **Invertebrates** (2) are animals that don't have bones inside their bodies.

Butterflies don't have bones.

Cows have a backbone.

Feeding habits

All animals have to eat food to live and grow. **Carnivores** (3) eat only meat. **Herbivores** (4). eat only plants. **Omnivores** (5) eat both meat and plants.

Humans eat meat and plants.

Ladybugs eat small insects.

Caterpillars eat only plants.

6 Read and complete the chart.

Snakes are covered with scales. Most snakes live on land, but some species live in the water. They have a backbone and eat other animals.

name	
body covering	scales
feeding habits	
physical structure	
place it lives	

7 Choose an animal to research. Then write and draw.

name	
body covering	
feeding habits	
physical structure	
place it lives	

8 Look at Activity 7 and complete. Then share your work.

1 The ______________ has ______________ (fur / scales / feathers / a shell).

2 It is a / an ______________ (carnivore / herbivore / omnivore).

3 It is a / an ______________ (vertebrate / invertebrate).

4 It is ______________ (terrestrial / aquatic).

UNIT 4

WHERE DOES FOOD COME FROM?

GEOGRAPHY

Look and circle.

These are **potatoes** / **tomatoes**.

UNIT 4

GEOGRAPHY

1 Write.

beans carrots cookies French fries
hamburgers ice pops onions pancakes
peppers potatoes sandwiches tomatoes

1  ____________

2  ____________

3  ____________

4  ____________

5  ____________

6  ____________

7  ____________

8  ____________

9  ____________

10  ____________

11  ____________

12  ____________

2 Circle the foods in Activity 1 that come straight from crops.

GLOSSARY

crop

TRACK 7

3 Listen and read.

What Is Crop Cultivation?

Crop cultivation is the process of producing food by growing certain plants. Some food crops consist of **grains**, **seeds and nuts**, **vegetables**, **fruits**, **herbs and spices**.

grains

seeds and nuts

vegetables

fruits

herbs and spices

4 Write which category each food belongs to.

1 

____

2 

____

3 

____

4 

____

5 

____

TRACK 8

5 Listen and read.

Livestock Farming

Livestock farming is the activity of raising animals to generate products that humans consume. Animals are raised to produce **meat**, **eggs**, **milk**, and **wool**.

meat

eggs

milk

wool

6 Match.

1 meat and milk	chicken
2 eggs	cow
3 wool	sheep

7 Look at the pictures. Write *C* (crop) or *L* (livestock).

1  ◯

2  ◯

3  ◯

4  ◯

GEOGRAPHY

8 Imagine you have a farm. Follow the steps below.

1 Complete the chart.

What animals do you want to raise?	What plants do you want to cultivate?
______________________	______________________
______________________	______________________
______________________	______________________
______________________	______________________
______________________	______________________

2 Draw the products made at your farm and label them.

livestock farming	crop cultivation

3 Explain your farm and its products to your classmates.

UNIT 5

MAKE-BELIEVE WORLD

ART

Look at the picture and circle.

The girl thinks she can **fly** / **swim**.

UNIT 5

ART

TRACK 9

1 Listen, read, and match.

My friend and I like to play make-believe. We like to pretend we can do things that we can't actually do.

Sometimes, I pretend I can **fly** (**1**) or **do taekwondo** (**2**). My friend likes to pretend he can **play the guitar** (**3**). What about you?

I pretend I can ________________

____________________________.

TRACK 10

2 Listen and read.

A theater is a place where a play is performed. It can be big or small, outdoors or indoors.

There is **visual language** like sets, costumes, images, and light. There are **sounds** like music, noises, and voices. There is **body language** like gesture, movements, and expressions. And there is **verbal language** like scripts and lines.

Indoor theater.

International Street Theater Festival in Krakow, Poland.

Think Twice

1 Circle.

Sets, costumes, images, and light are **visual** / **verbal** language.

2 Do you like theater?

3 Play Sound and Action!

4 Play Transformation of Objects! Use your body, make sounds, and do an action.

1

2

5 Play a miming game. Pretend you are one of the objects below.

blender

cup

hanger

6 Think about an object. Play a miming game with your classmates.

7 Read the beginning of a story. Write two different sequences. Act the scenes out.

Allison invents a spaceship to go to the moon. When she gets there, she ...

1 ____

____

2 ____

____

UNIT

6

IT'S TIME TO RELAX

HISTORY

Look at the picture and circle.

They are playing **board games** / **soccer** / **computer games.**

UNIT 6

HISTORY

1 Unscramble the words to make sentences. Then match the sentences to the pictures.

1 to likes She music listening *She likes listening to music*.
2 playing like They games board ________________.
3 reading books likes She ________________.
4 drawing He likes ________________.
5 like They dancing ________________.
6 TV They watching like ________________.

2 Where do you do these activities? Check (✓) your answers in the chart.

activity	in your house	in outdoor areas
draw		
read books		
play soccer		
listen to music		
watch TV		
dance		
play board games		

TRACK 11

3 Listen and read.

Public and Private Spaces

There are **public** and **private spaces** within a city.

A public space is an area that is open and accessible for people to use. **Public parks**, **squares**, and **beaches** are examples of public spaces.

A private space is a place that people don't have free access to. **Your house** is an example of a private space.

A beach in Spain.

A house in Brazil.

Think Twice

1 Read and circle.

Your grandma's house is a public / private space.

The beach is a public / private space.

2 Can you name other public spaces?

4 Look at the pictures and complete the sentences with *public* or *private*.

1 This square in Argentina is a ________________ area.

2 This swimming pool is ________________.

UNIT 6

HISTORY

TRACK 12

5 Listen and read. Then number.

Leisure Activities

People do leisure activities in their free time. They can have a lot of fun!

There are many **public places** (1) for people to have fun and relax. Beaches, parks, and museums are some of them.

People also enjoy their free time at **home** (2), doing puzzles, reading a book, or watching TV.

Leisure activities in the past and now

Making time for leisure is a very old practice. **In the past** (3), people used to spend their free time outdoors, in public areas. The Greeks, for example, listened to music in open-air theaters.

People still do outdoor activities **today** (4). But they spend more time at home because of technology. They can watch movies, play virtual games, or tour a museum without leaving their houses.

Mother and daughter doing puzzles.

People visiting a museum.

A person playing a virtual reality game.

An ancient theater in Greece.

6 Match and say.

1 People can enjoy their free time …

2 In the past, people used to spend more time …

3 Today people spend more time …

a at home.

b outdoors, in public areas.

c in public or private spaces.

7 Complete the chart for you.

	free time activities	total
public space		
private space		

8 Look at Activity 7. Create a bar graph and share it with your classmates.

WHERE DO I SPEND MOST OF MY FREE TIME?

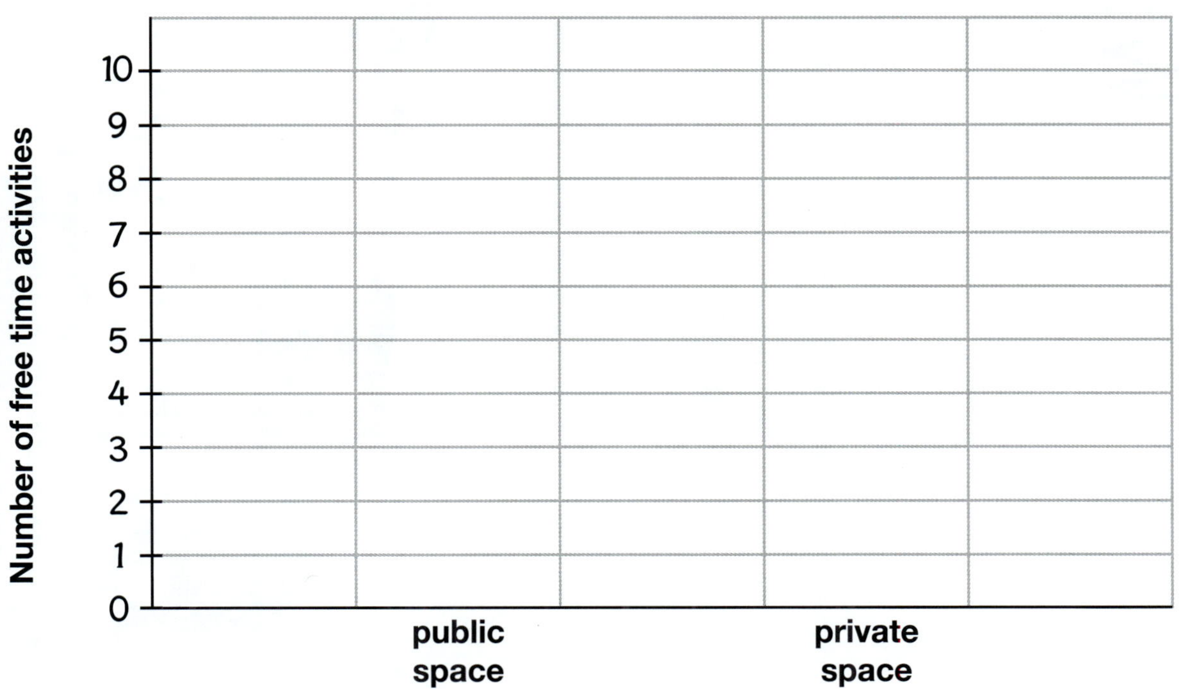

UNIT 7

'WHERE DO YOU LIVE?'

GEOGRAPHY
Look and complete.
This is a big ________
in Mongolia.

UNIT 7

GEOGRAPHY

1 Complete the crossword.

1 H

2 B T

3

4 C

5 C

6 A

2 Where can we find the places from Activity 1?

city	country

TRACK 13

3 Listen and read.

The Country

In the country, you can find fields, forests, farms, and **country houses**. The houses are far from each other. There aren't many streets, stores, or factories. There are less people than in the cities and many people work in **crop** or **livestock** farming. The products of these activities are often celebrated in **festivals**.

Country house in the United Kingdom.

Grape festival in Spain.

Crop cultivation in China.

Livestock farming in Mongolia.

Think Twice

1 Where do people usually work in the country?

2 Can you think of a leisure activity people do in the country?

UNIT 7

GEOGRAPHY

TRACK 14

4 Listen and read.

The City

Cities have lots of streets, stores, and buildings. There are many people from different origins in cities. They usually work in **industry**, **trade**, or in **services**.

In the industry sector, factories generate products for human consumption. Trade is the activity of buying and selling things. And people who work in services can be doctors, cleaners, electricians, lawyers, etc. Cities offer several leisure options, like parks, movie theaters, and sports complexes.

Industry in South Africa.

Trading at a market in Denmark.

Dog walking service in Australia.

Think Twice

1 Where do people usually work in the cities?

2 Can you think of a leisure activity people do in the city?

GEOGRAPHY

5 Let's research!

	big city	small town in the country
name		
country		
population		
leisure activities		
economy (Where do people work?)		

6 Act out and guess!

UNIT 8

LISTENING TO MUSIC

ART

Look and answer.

What instrument is the girl playing?

She is playing the ______________.

UNIT 8

ART

1 Label the instruments. Use the words from the box.

trumpet	violin	drum	recorder	tambourine	guitar

TRACK 15

2 Listen and write.

1 

____

2 

____

3 

____

4 

____

5 

____

6 

____

TRACK 16

3 Listen and number.

Music Genres

Music is an important form of art and national culture. It affects our emotions and our body.
There are many kinds of music, and you can recognize them by their rhythm, type of instrument, and ethnic origin.
Some examples of popular music genres are **rock** (1), **country** (2), **dance** (3), and **Latin music** (4).

Band playing country music in Luckenbach, Texas, USA.

Members of a samba school in Santa Catarina, Brazil.

Rock music band performing on the street in Vilnius, Lithuania.

DJ playing for dancing people in Hamburg, Germany.

Think Twice

1 Read and circle.

Music is a form of art. True / False

Music genres are all the same. True / False

Instruments are important in music. True/ False

2 Do you know another music genre? Which one?

UNIT 8

ART

TRACK 17

4 Listen and check (✓).

dance music ◯ rock music ◯ Latin music ◯ country music ◯

Can you identify any instruments in the music?

TRACK 18

5 Listen and read.

Music is part of everyday life. It can influence our moods and behaviors. Our preferences in music show our values and views of the world.

It is also a way of communication. We can share emotions, intentions, and stories through music. It's a very important way of communication for people with special needs. How do you feel when you listen to music?

6 Read and write.

1 What's one new thing you discovered about music?

____.

2 How is music used in your home, school, and community?

____.

ART

7 Research about a band you like.

name	
music genre	
country	
instruments used	
famous songs	
why you like them	
places where you usually listen to the songs	

8 Draw and write.

I usually listen to music to ______________________________.

UNIT 9

NUMBER LINE

MATH

Look at the picture and check (✓).

What is the next number on the racetrack?

9 ○   11 ○   10 ○

UNIT 9

MATH

1 Write the missing numbers and words. Then say.

10		30		50
ten	twenty	______	forty	______
60			90	100
______	seventy	eighty	______	______

2 Add and write.

1 20  + 40  = There are 60 buses.

2 10  + 30  = There are ______________.

3 10  + 10  = There are ______________.

4 40  + 30  = There are ______________.

3 Complete with the numbers you found in Activity 2, writing them in order. Then check (✓).

10 — [ ] — 30 — [ ] — 50 — [60] — [ ] — 80

This line goes up in ◯ 2s. ◯ 5s. ◯ 10s.

TRACK 19

4 Listen and read.

Number Line

A number line is a straight line with numbers written in order and at **regular intervals**. It can show any number sequence: from 1 to 10, from 1 to 100, etc. It also can be numbered in 1s, 2s, 5s, 10s, and so on.

The position of each number is indicated by a **mark**. The **numbers increase** as we move **from left to right** and **decrease** on moving **from right to left**.

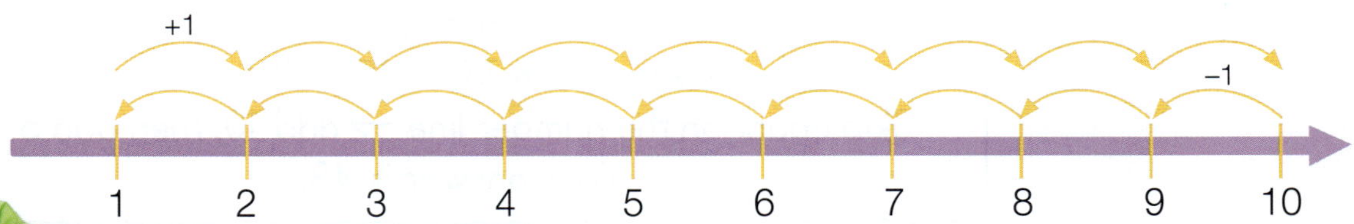

smaller ← → bigger

Think Twice

1 Read and circle.

A number line is a straight line with any number sequence. True / False

It has numbers at irregular intervals. True / False

2 Can you name a real-life example of a number line?

5 Solve the riddles. Use the number line.

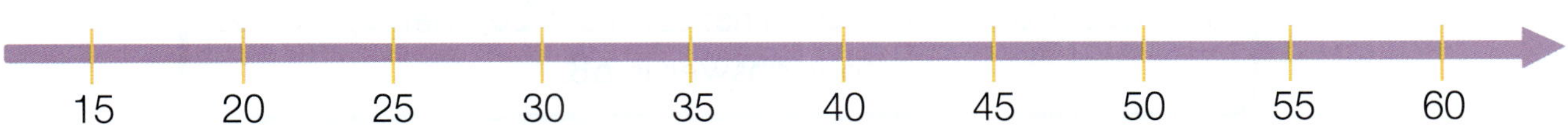

1 Start on number 15. Jump forward 3 times and find me. What number am I?

2 Start on number 55. Jump backward twice and find me. What number am I?

TRACK 20

6 Listen and read.

Add and Subtract on a Number Line

Use the number line for **addition** and **subtraction** operations.

Addition: jump spaces **forwards** – from the left to the right. Check the example.

Operation: 28 + 15 = ______
Start at 28.
Decompose 15 → 15 = 10 + 5
Skip count on the number line → add 10, then add 5.
Your answer is 43.

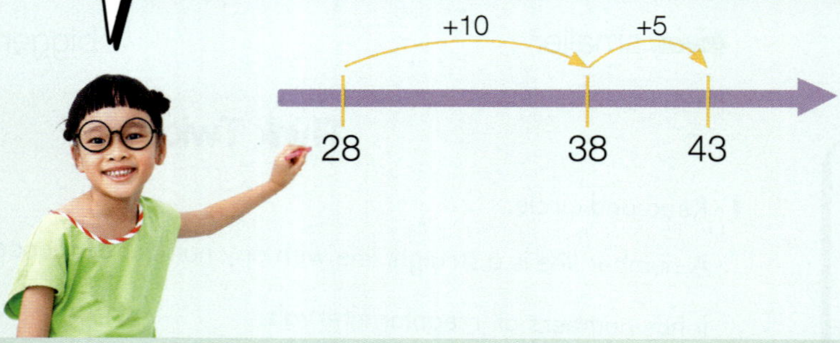

Subtraction: jump spaces **backwards** – from the right to the left. Check the example:

Operation: 95 – 27 = ______
Start at 95.
Decompose 27 → 27 = 20 + 5 + 2
Skip count on the number line: subtract 20, then 5, then 2.
Your answer is 68.

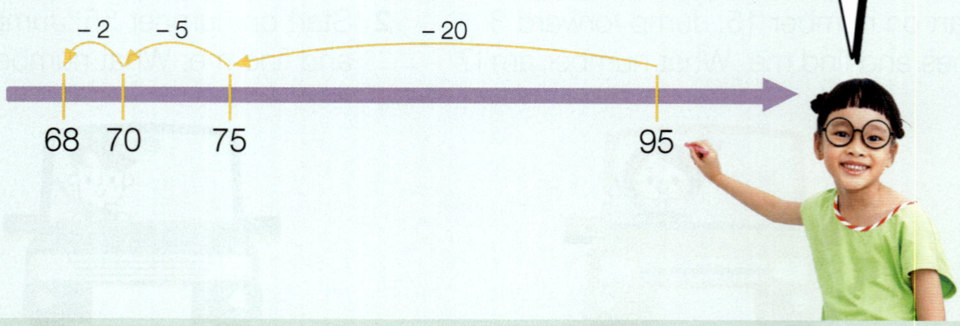

7 Solve the problems using the number lines.

1 Barbara is traveling to New York. The train ticket costs $48. The bus ticket costs $18. How much will she spend?

Answer: ________ dollars.

2 Sam had 57 cookies. He gave 28 to his friend John. How many cookies are left?

Answer: ________ cookies.

8 Create and solve an addition or subtraction problem. Use the items below.

____

____

____

Answer: ____.

UNIT 10

MY COMMUNITY

HISTORY

Read and circle.

The boys are wearing traditional costumes. True / False

They belong to different communities. True / False

UNIT 10

HISTORY

TRACK 21

1 Read and complete. Then listen and check your answers.

~~big~~ hats old long pants shirts skirts small

Titicaca is a ____big____ and high lake between Bolivia and Peru. Many traditional communities live on ____________ artificial islands on it. The Uros people form an ____________ community that depends on fishing, hunting, and selling crafts to tourists. They produce ____________ boats out of the same plant used to build the islands.

Their traditional clothes are very colorful. Women usually wear ____________ and jackets and men wear ____________ and ____________. They all wear ____________ as a form of sun protection.

Uros girl in traditional clothes.

Uros men in traditional clothes producing craft hats.

The boats and the islands are made from the *totora* plant.

HISTORY

TRACK 22

2 Listen and read.

What Is a Community?

We live among many people. Some of them are really close to us and share the same house, like our family. Others share the same space, like our school, building, neighborhood, or village, but are not necessarily part of our family.

A community is formed by people that live nearby, people that share common characteristics and interests, or people that have the same origin.

A city holds a lot of communities. In the suburbs, countryside, or villages, there are fewer communities and they are not close to each other.

In each community, different groups of people perform different activities to provide the things that everyone needs.

Chinatown is the home of the Chinese community in New York.

Teenagers painting a community art mural in England.

People working on their community garden in South Africa.

Maori community performing a traditional dance in New Zealand.

Think Twice

1 Is a city formed by one or by more than one community?

2 Do all members of a community have the same occupation?

UNIT 10

HISTORY

TRACK 23

3 Listen and read. Then look at the pictures and write *sea*, *farm*, or *urban*.

A Community by the Sea

Lobitos is a small town on the north coast of Peru. Many people who live in Lobitos work as fishermen. They fish using traditional methods and help each other a lot. During vacation seasons, the town is also full of surfers from all over the world. Some of them teach the local children how to surf.

A Farming Community

In the Peruvian town of Maras, many people work in farms. Some of them cultivate corn and potatoes. Others extract salt from the water. There are also people who sell the goods produced by the farmers in the local market.

Urban Communities

There are over 8 million inhabitants in the capital of Peru, Lima. It is a very big city, with lots of different communities. In the neighborhood of Miraflores, for example, retired people get together every Saturday to dance salsa in a local park. Some teenagers meet up to go skating after school.

1 

____

2 

____

3 

____

4 

____

5 

____

6 

____

HISTORY

4 Answer the questions below. Then share it with a classmate.

1 Look back at Activity 3. Which community is the most similar to yours?

____

2 Is your community traditional?

____

3 Is it a big or small community?

____

4 Do you wear similar or traditional clothes? What kind?

____

5 What do you like the most about your community?

____

5 Draw a scene that represents your community. Share it with a classmate.

Director of Languages Brazil: Patrícia Souza De Luccia
Publishing Manager and Field Researcher: Patricia Muradas
Content Creation Coordinator: Cristina do Vale
Art Editor: Jean Aranha
Content Development: Ana Elisa Martins
Content Editors: Ana Beatriz da Costa Moreira, Daniela Gonçala da Costa, Luciana Pereira da Silva
Digital Editor: Ana Paula Girardi
Editorial Assistant: Roberta Somera
Editorial Intern: Bruna Marques
Art Assistant: Denis Araujo
Art Intern: Jacqueline Alves
Graphic Production: Tatiane Romano, Thais Mendes P. Galvão
Proofreaders: Edward Willson, Márcia Leme, Sabrina Cairo Bileski
Design Concept: Design Divertido Artes Gráficas
Page Make-Up: Figurattiva Editorial
Photo Research: Marcia Sato
Image Processing: Jean Aranha, Jacqueline Alves, Denis Araujo
Audio: Argila Music, Núcleo de Criação
Cover Concept: Jean Aranha
Cover photography: Nadezhda1906/iStockphoto/Getty Images, anilakkus/iStockphoto/Getty Images, Bubert/iStockphoto/Getty Images, LokFung/iStockphoto/Getty Images, Photoco/iStockphoto/Getty Images
Illustrations: Gustavo Gialuca (p. 13, 14, 20, 32, 33, 54, 55, 57), Jim Peacock (p. 12), Melanie Sharpe | Sylvie Poggio Artists Agency (p. 18).

We would like to dedicate this book to teachers all over Brazil. We would also like to thank our clients and teachers who have helped us make this book better with their many rich contributions and feedback straight from the classroom!

The authors and publishers would like to thank the following for permission to reproduce the photographic material:

p. 4: guenterguni/iStockphoto/Getty Images, deebrowning/iStockphoto/Getty Images, elkor/iStockphoto/Getty Images; p. 6: Pollyana Ventura/iStockphoto/Getty Images, whitemay/iStockphoto/Getty Images, innovatedcaptures/iStockphoto/Getty Images, FatCamera/iStockphoto/Getty Images, yulkapopkova/iStockphoto/Getty Images, aroundtheworld.photography/iStockphoto/Getty Images, Deagreez/iStockphoto/Getty Images, DavidCallan/iStockphoto/Getty Images; p. 7: Windzepher/iStockphoto/Getty Images, ermess/iStockphoto/Getty Images, Sergio Capuzzimati/iStockphoto/Getty Images, CharlieTong/iStockphoto/Getty Images; p. 8: Ohad Falik, mofles/iStockphoto/Getty Images, chameleonseye/iStockphoto/Getty Images, gpointstudio/iStockphoto/Getty Images, kieferpix/iStockphoto/Getty Images, master1305/iStockphoto/Getty Images; p. 10: coffeekai/iStockphoto/Getty Images; p. 13: BreakingTheWalls/iStockphoto/Getty Images, Alex Belomlinsky/iStockphoto/Getty Images; p. 16: WLDavies/iStockphoto/Getty Images; p. 19: Krisztian Juhasz/iStockphoto/Getty Images, PrinPrince/iStockphoto/Getty Images, Mark Kostich/iStockphoto/Getty Images, ArmanWerthPhotography/iStockphoto/Getty Images, GlobalP/iStockphoto/Getty Images, georgeclerk/iStockphoto/Getty Images; p. 20: biscotto87/iStockphoto/Getty Images, fireflamenco/iStockphoto/Getty Images, JungleOutThere/iStockphoto/Getty Images, naveen0301/iStockphoto/Getty Images, DutchScenery/iStockphoto/Getty Images, andresr/iStockphoto/Getty Images, Jonathan Austin Daniels/iStockphoto/Getty Images, AttaBoyLuther/iStockphoto/Getty Images; p. 21: Byronsdad/iStockphoto/Getty Images; p. 22: firemanYU/iStockphoto/Getty Images; p. 24: Andrey Elkin/iStockphoto/Getty Images, kaanates/iStockphoto/Getty Images, Bozena_Fulawka/iStockphoto/Getty Images, Hyrma/iStockphoto/Getty Images, AlasdairJames/iStockphoto/Getty Images, Hyrma/iStockphoto/Getty Images, nitrub/iStockphoto/Getty Images, subjug/iStockphoto/Getty Images, posteriori/iStockphoto/Getty Images, rclassenlayouts/iStockphoto/Getty Images, YinYang/iStockphoto/Getty Images, Barcin/iStockphoto/Getty Images, dszc/iStockphoto/Getty Images; p. 25: malerapaso/iStockphoto/Getty Images, fcafotodigital/iStockphoto/Getty Images, clubfoto/iStockphoto/Getty Images, aluxum/iStockphoto/Getty Images, monticelllo/iStockphoto/Getty Images, julichka/iStockphoto/Getty Images, Magone/iStockphoto/Getty Images, rimglow/iStockphoto/Getty Images, anna1311/iStockphoto/Getty Images, eyewave/iStockphoto/Getty Images; p. 26: AlexRaths/iStockphoto/Getty Images, GCapture/iStockphoto/Getty Images, Sezeryadigar/iStockphoto/Getty Images, gornostaj/iStockphoto/Getty Images, tomazl/iStockphoto/Getty Images, NNehring/iStockphoto/Getty Images, PeopleImages/iStockphoto/Getty Images, GomezDavid/iStockphoto/Getty Images; p. 28: FG Trade/iStockphoto/Getty Images; p. 30: AleksandarGeorgiev/iStockphoto/Getty Images, zdravinjo/iStockphoto/Getty Images, LightFieldStudios/iStockphoto/Getty Images; p. 31: Richard Lewisohn/iStockphoto/Getty Images, wjarek/iStockphoto/Getty Images; p. 32: ONYXprj/iStockphoto/Getty Images, ONYXprj/iStockphoto/Getty Images, Coprid/iStockphoto/Getty Images, rimglow/iStockphoto/Getty Images; p. 33: rolfbodmer/iStockphoto/Getty Images, EugeneTomeev/iStockphoto/Getty Images, UserGI15633745/iStockphoto/Getty Images, tostphoto/iStockphoto/Getty Images; p. 34: Wavebreakmedia/iStockphoto/Getty Images; p. 36: FatCamera/iStockphoto/Getty Images, gradyreese/iStockphoto/Getty Images, Imgorthand/iStockphoto/Getty Images, OJO Images/iStockphoto/Getty Images, vgajic/iStockphoto/Getty Images, Stígur Már Karlsson /Heimsmyndir/iStockphoto/Getty Images; p. 37: Mauro_Repossini/iStockphoto/Getty Images, aprott/iStockphoto/Getty Images, Juan Jose Napuri/iStockphoto/Getty Images, PeopleImages/iStockphoto/Getty Images, uschools/iStockphoto/Getty Images, mihtiander/iStockphoto/Getty Images, piovesempre/iStockphoto/Getty Images; p. 38: monkeybusinessimages/iStockphoto/Getty Images, monkeybusinessimages/iStockphoto/Getty Images, Damir Khabirov/iStockphoto/Getty Images, zoroasto/iStockphoto/Getty Images p. 40: tanukiphoto/iStockphoto/Getty Images; p. 42: Maksymowicz/iStockphoto/Getty Images, kodachrome25/iStockphoto/Getty Images, Marcus Lindstrom/iStockphoto/Getty Images, castenoid/iStockphoto/Getty Images, Rainbow79/iStockphoto/Getty Images, Drimafilm/iStockphoto/Getty Images; p. 43: Peter Llewellyn/iStockphoto/Getty Images, kiko_jimenez/iStockphoto/Getty Images, Chaiyaporn1144/iStockphoto/Getty Images, Goddard_Photography/iStockphoto/Getty Images; p. 44: Wavebreakmedia/iStockphoto/Getty Images, anouchka/iStockphoto/Getty Images, yellowsarah/iStockphoto/Getty Images; p. 45: adamkaz/iStockphoto/Getty Images; p. 46: ajkkafe/iStockphoto/Getty Images; p. 48: Highwaystarz-Photography/iStockphoto/Getty Images, forrest9/iStockphoto/Getty Images, moniaphoto/iStockphoto/Getty Images, pepifoto/iStockphoto/Getty Images, Kailash Kumar/iStockphoto/Getty Images, Lebazele/iStockphoto/Getty Images, JUN2/iStockphoto/Getty Images.

Dados Internacionais de Catalogação na Publicação (CIP)

Bibliotecária responsável: Aline Graziele Benitez CRB-1/3129

M294n Martins, Ana Elisa Teixeira
1.ed. Next Station CLIL Book 2 / Ana Elisa Teixeira Martins. – 1.ed. – São Paulo: Macmillan Education do Brasil, 2020.
64 p.; il.; 21 x 27 cm. – (Coleção Next Station)

ISBN: 978-85-511-0148-3 (aluno)
978-85-511-0153-7 (professor)

1. Língua inglesa. I. Título.

Índice para catálogo sistemático:
1. Língua inglesa

MACMILLAN EDUCATION DO BRASIL
Av. Brigadeiro Faria Lima, 1.309, 3° Andar – Jd. Paulistano – São Paulo – SP – 01452-002
www.macmillan.com.br
Customer Service: [55] (11) 4613-2278
0800 16 88 77
Fax: [55] (11) 4612-6098
Printed in Brazil. First print. July, 2019.
Impresso na EGB, 03 2024.